Jenny Kee's Needlepoint Designs

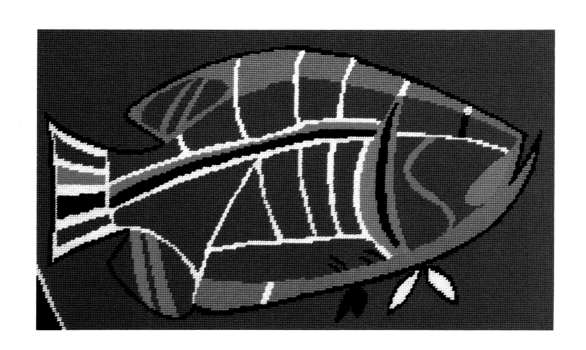

Jenny Kee's Needlepoint Designs

INSTRUCTIONS AND PATTERNS BY ALISON SNEPP

CASSELL

A CASSELL BOOK

First published in the UK 1993
by Cassell
Villiers House 41/47 Strand London WC2N 5JE

First published in Australia in 1993
by Simon & Schuster Australia

British Library Cataloguing-in-Publication Data
A catalogue record for this book is available from the British Library

ISBN 0-304-34321-8

Photography by Rodney Weidland
Styling by Jean Wright
Designed by Jack Jagtenberg
Illustrations by Graeme Nichols
Typeset in Australia by Asset Typesetting Pty Ltd
Produced by Mandarin Offset in Hong Kong
Printed in China

NOTE: Because of the complicated nature of some of the graphs it may be advisable to work
from enlarged photocopies.

Contents

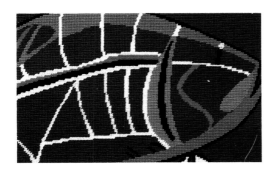

The Sea

The Earth

Harmony

General Instructions

ACKNOWLEDGEMENTS

Jenny Kee would like to thank the following people: Alison Snepp, Kirsty Melville and Elenie Poulos from Simon & Schuster, Jean Wright, Rodney Weidland, Jack Jagtenberg, Louise Bishop and my mother Enid Kee.

Alison Snepp would like to thank the people who assisted in the production of the projects. DMC Needlecraft so generously provided all the wools and canvas for the embroideries. My enthusiastic team of embroiderers were Kerry, Joan J., Pat, Christina, Patricia and Joan T. The assembly of the projects was carefully completed by Mary, and John took meticulous care in drawing most of the charts. Thanks also to Kirsty Melville and Elenie Poulos of Simon & Schuster for their understanding and patience throughout the project.

Simon & Schuster Australia would like to thank the management and staff of Appley Hoare Antiques and The Bathers Pavilion restaurant for their kind assistance with locations and props.

PICTURE CREDITS

Jonathan Chester/Extreme Images — pages 5, 22, 32, 38, 42, 45, 48, 57, 68, 72, 76, 84, 93
Kevin Deacon/Dive 2000 — pages 8-9, 10, 18
Philip Quirk/Wildlight — page 26
David Moore/Wildlight — pages 36-37
Austral International — pages 60, 66-67, 80
Grenville Turner/Wildlight — page 63
All other photographs by Rodney Weidland

PREFACE

Since 1974 when I first started designing graphic knitwear, my work has expanded in many different directions. In 1977 I moved into fabric design, from there to rugs and scarves and, most recently, into homewear such as bed linen, napery and ceramics. And my product range continues to grow.

So after two successful knitting books, it is exciting for me to be producing a needlepoint book. It is exciting both because it heralds further new directions in my work and because needlepoint is at the forefront of the current upsurge in interest in traditional crafts. People are searching for pastimes that reflect a deeper desire for peace and comfort and a growing appreciation for all that is natural. Traditional crafts such as needlepoint are, therefore, well suited to my designs — nature and harmony being the constant sources of my inspiration.

I have to be close to nature and I really cherish the earth. My view of the world is strong, spontaneous, bold and optimistic and the colourful, graphic designs in this book reflect my vision. I hope that through my work you will be inspired to help preserve our natural environment and encourage unity and harmony everywhere.

Jenny Kee

The Sea

BARRIER REEF

Materials

Zweigart canvas 48 threads/10 cm
(12 threads/in), a piece 51 x 51 cm
(20 x 20 in).

DMC Tapestry Wool Article 486 in the
following colours and quantities:

3 skeins	purple	7243
4 skeins	yellow	7434
5 skeins	aqua	7807
4 skeins	red	7544
4 skeins	blue	7797
3 skeins	orange	7850
3 skeins	green	7342
2 skeins	black	
3 skeins	hot pink	7602
1 skein	white	

Tapestry needle, size 22.

50 cm (19¾ in) aqua medium-weight cotton
fabric for the piping, and backing the cushion.

1.5 m (1²/₃ yd) cotton piping cord.

Size of finished embroidery: 31 x 31 cm
(12¼ x 12¼ in).

Instructions

Prepare and mount the canvas on to a roller
frame as shown in the General Instructions on
page 94.

Measure 10 cm (4 in) and 10 cm (4 in)
down from the top left-hand corner of the
canvas. This point corresponds with the top
left-hand stitch on the chart. Start the
embroidery here. One square on the chart
represents one stitch on the canvas. Each
symbol represents a colour of the tapestry
wool as shown on the key to the chart.

Work the canvas using half cross-stitch as
shown in Needlepoint Techniques on
page 100.

When the stitching is complete, block the
canvas following instructions on page 95, and
make up the embroidery into a piped cushion
according to the instructions on page 99.

BARRIER REEF

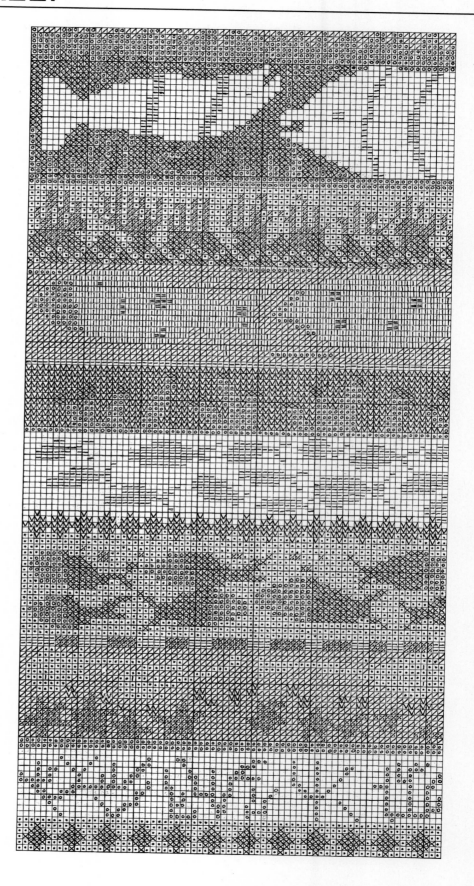

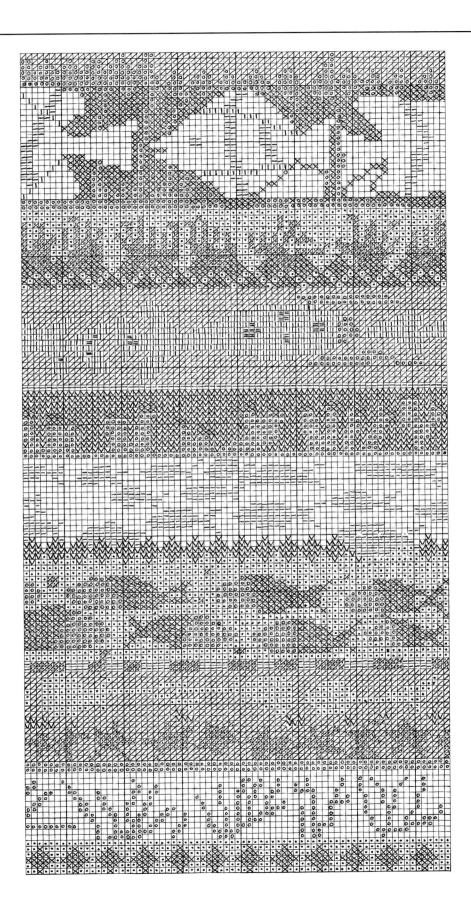

APHRODITE

Materials

Zweigart canvas 48 threads/10 cm
(12 threads/in), a piece 53 x 53 cm
(20¾ x 20¾ in).

DMC Tapestry Wool Article 486 in the
following colours and quantities:

5 skeins royal blue	7796
3 skeins turquoise	7596
6 skeins mauve	7896
8 skeins aqua	7597
5 skeins coral	7760
4 skeins pink	7204
6 skeins yellow	7473
4 skeins hot pink	7602

Tapestry needle, size 22.

50 cm (19¾ in) blue medium-weight cotton
fabric for the piping, and backing the cushion.

1.5 m (1²/₃ yd) cotton piping cord.

Size of finished embroidery: 33.5 x 32.8 cm
(13¼ x 13 in).

Instructions

Prepare and mount the canvas on to a roller
frame as shown in the General Instructions on
page 94.

Measure 10 cm (4 in) in and 10 cm (4 in)
down from the top left-hand corner of the
canvas. This point corresponds with the top
left-hand stitch on the chart. Start the
embroidery here. One square on the chart
represents one stitch on the canvas. Each
symbol represents a colour of the tapestry
wool as shown on the key to the chart.

Work the canvas using half cross-stitch as
shown in Needlepoint Techniques on
page 100.

When the stitching is complete, block the
canvas following instructions on page 95, and
make up the embroidery into a piped cushion
according to the instructions on page 99.

APHRODITE

TROPICAL SEA GARDEN

Materials

Zweigart canvas 48 threads/10 cm
(12 threads/in), a piece 55 x 59 cm
(21½ x 23¼ in).

DMC Tapestry Wool Article 486 in the
following colours and quantities:

5 skeins	mid blue	7797
2 skeins	emerald	7345
1 skein	gold	7436
5 skeins	citrus yellow	7725
3 skeins	red	7544
5 skeins	purple	7175
6 skeins	dark blue	7791
4 skeins	orange	7439
5 skeins	pale blue	7996
4 skeins	pink	7600
2 skeins	lime green	7341

Tapestry needle, size 22.

50 cm (19¾ in) navy blue medium-weight
cotton fabric for the piping, and backing the
cushion.

1.8 m (2 yd) cotton piping cord.

Size of finished embroidery: 34.5 x 38.5 cm
(13½ x 15¼ in).

Instructions

Prepare and mount the canvas on to a roller
frame as shown in the General Instructions on
page 94.

Holding the canvas so that the shorter side
is along the top, measure 10 cm (4 in) in and
10 cm (4 in) down from the top left-hand
corner of the canvas. This point corresponds
with the top left-hand stitch on the chart. Start
the embroidery here. One square on the
chart represents one stitch on the canvas.
Each symbol represents a colour of the
tapestry wool as shown on the key to the
chart.

Work the canvas using half cross-stitch as
shown in Needlepoint Techniques on page
100.

When the stitching is complete, block the
canvas following instructions on page 95, and
make up the embroidery into a piped cushion
as shown on page 99.

TROPICAL SEA GARDEN

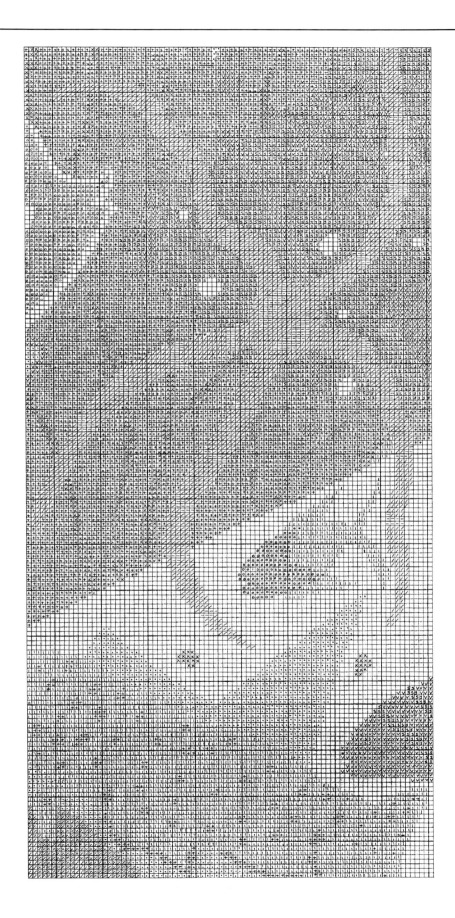

KEY

☐	7797
☒	7345
⊠	7436
⊙	7725
⟋	7544
S	7175
+	7791
I	7439
—	7996
•	7600
V	7341

SPOTTY FISH

Materials

Zweigart canvas 48 threads/10 cm
(12 threads/in), a piece 49 x 46 cm
(19⅓ x 18¼ in).

DMC Tapestry Wool Article 486 in the
following colours and quantities:

4 skeins blue	7317
3 skeins pink	7600
2 skeins white	
3 skeins orange	7947
1 skein emerald	7915
5 skeins gold	7436
3 skeins black	
4 skeins lime green	7342
2 skeins red	7666
2 skeins purple	7157

Tapestry needle, size 22.

70 cm (27½ in) black and white spotted
medium-weight cotton fabric for the cushion
backing and frame.

30 cm (11¾ in) black medium-weight cotton
fabric for the piping.

1.8 m (2 yd) cotton piping cord.

Size of finished embroidery: 29 x 26 cm
(11½ x 10¼ in).

Instructions

Prepare and mount the canvas on to a roller
frame as shown in the General Instructions on
page 94.

Measure 10 cm (4 in) in and 10 cm (4 in)
down from the top left-hand corner of the
canvas. This point corresponds with the top
left-hand stitch on the chart. Start the
embroidery here. One square on the chart
represents one stitch on the canvas. Each
symbol represents a colour of the tapestry
wool as shown on the key to the chart.

Work the canvas using half cross-stitch as
shown in Needlepoint Techniques on
page 100.

When the stitching is complete, block the
canvas following instructions on page 95 and
make up the embroidery into a framed, piped
cushion according to the instructions on
page 98.

KEY

☐	**7807**
☒	**black**
▨	**white**
•	**7318**
◦	**7439**

DOLPHINS

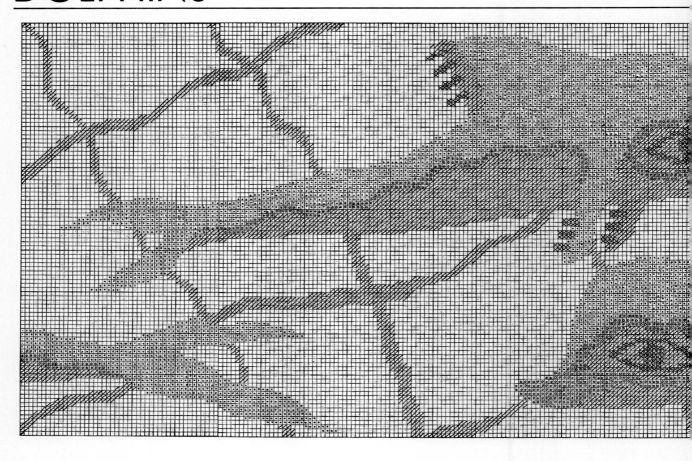

AFTER THE FIRE

COUNTRY

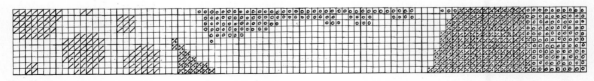

base

handle

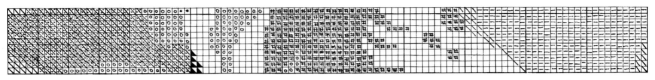

join A to A   A

A   join B to B   B

B   join C to C   C

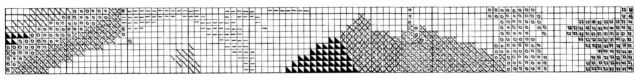

C

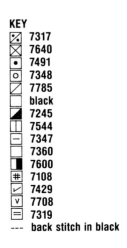

KEY

⊠⦁	7317
⊠	7640
⦁	7491
○	7348
╱	7785
	black
◣	7245
▥	7544
─	7347
	7360
◼	7600
⊞	7108
⌴	7429
v	7708
⊟	7319
---	back stitch in black

Assembly of the shoulder bag

From the black cotton fabric cut two squares 45 x 45 cm (17¾ x 17¾ in) for the bag faces, one strip 9 cm x 45 cm (3½ x 17¾ in) for the base, and one strip 9 cm x 1.7 m (3½ in x 1¾ yd) for the handle. From the remaining black fabric cut 5 m (5½ yd) bias and make the bias into piping according to the instructions on page 96.

Pin the piping to each long edge of the embroidery for the bag handle. Machine sew the piping into place, stitching close to the piping cord. Cut off excess piping beyond embroidery. Pin the remaining piping along the top edge of the embroidery on each bag face. Machine sew the piping into place close to the piping cord. Cut off excess piping beyond the embroidery. *Note:* when the piping is being pinned to the embroidery the cord side of the piping should lie along the edge of the embroidery and the raw edges of the piping should be closest to the raw edge of the canvas.

Hint: check that the piping has been attached in the correct position by folding back the canvas after the piping has been pinned to the edge of the embroidery. If any white canvas is visible, re-position the piping so that it sits absolutely along the edge of the embroidery.

Pin the bottom edge of one bag face to a long edge of the base with right sides together. Machine sew the base and bag face together. Pin the bottom edge of the second bag face to the other long edge of the base with right sides together and machine sew.

Starting at the bottom corner where the bag face and the base join, pin the handle to the side of the bag face with the right sides together. Machine stitch the handle to the side of the bag face close to the cord in the piping. *Note:* this seam will not extend along the length of the handle but only up one side of the bag face.

Pin the other end of the same piped side of the handle to the other side of the bag face where it joins the base, checking that the handle is not twisted. Machine stitch the handle to the side of the bag face, making sure the stitching is very close to the piping cord.

Pin the other piped side of the handle to the other face of the bag, starting where the bag face and base have been joined. The right sides of the embroidery should be facing each other. Machine stitch the seam very close to the piping cord.

Pin and machine stitch together the short ends of the base and the handle. Turn the assembled shoulder bag right side out.

To assemble the lining, pin the bottom edge of a bag face lining section to a long side of the base lining with right sides together. Machine sew the seam using a 2.5 cm (1 in) seam allowance. Pin the bottom edge of the other bag face lining to the other long edge of the base lining, still using a 2.5 cm (1 in) seam allowance. Machine stitch the seam. *Note:* a 2.5 cm (1 in) seam allowance has been allowed on all lining sections.

Starting at the point where a bag face lining joins the base lining, pin the long side of the handle lining to the side of the bag face lining with right sides together. Machine stitch the seam to a point 2.5 cm (1 in) below the top of the bag face lining. Starting at the other end of the same side pin the handle lining to the other side of the bag face lining starting at the point where the bag face lining joins the base lining. Machine stitch the seam stopping 2.5 cm (1 in) below the top edge of the bag face lining.

Join the other bag face lining to the other side of the handle lining in the same manner. Stitch the base lining to the handle lining along the short edges of both pieces of lining.

Place the assembled lining into the assembled shoulder bag, matching seams. Turn back the seam allowances on the embroidered section of the bag handle and the corresponding section of the handle lining so that the lining will fit neatly behind the piped handle. Pin together and slip-stitch using black machine thread.

Turn down the seam allowance on the top piped edge of each bag face. Turn down the seam allowances on the top edge of each bag face lining to match the embroidery. Pin the folds together and slip-stitch.

WARATAH

Materials

Zweigart canvas 48 threads/10 cm
(12 threads/in), a piece 50 x 50 cm
(19¾ x 19¾ in).

DMC Tapestry Wool Article 486 in the
following colours and quantities:

5 skeins black		
8 skeins bright blue	7995	
1 skein dark red	7210	
6 skeins red	7666	
3 skeins very dark green	7701	

Tapestry needle, size 22.

Size of finished embroidery: 23.8 x 29.8 cm
(9⅓ x 11¾ in).

Instructions

Prepare and mount the canvas on to a roller
frame as shown in the General Instructions on
page 94.

Measure 10 cm (4 in) in and 10 cm (4 in)
down from the top left-hand corner of the
canvas. This point corresponds with the top
left-hand stitch on the chart. Start the
embroidery here. One square on the chart
represents one stitch on the canvas. Each
symbol represents a colour of tapestry wool
as shown on the key to the chart.

Work the canvas using half cross-stitch as
shown in Needlepoint Techniques on
page 100.

When the stitching is complete, block the
canvas following the directions on page 95,
and have it professionally framed.

WARATAH

KEY

+	black
•	black
	7995
−	7210
o	7666
\	7701

59

BLACK OPAL

Materials

Zweigart canvas 48 threads/10 cm
(12 threads/in), a piece 45 x 45 cm
(17¾ x 17¾ in).

DMC Tapestry Wool Article 486 in the
following colours and quantities:

3 skeins	mid blue	7317
2 skeins	yellow	7725
4 skeins	red	7544
2 skeins	jacaranda	7708
2 skeins	dark blue	7336
3 skeins	dark maroon	7139
4 skeins	purple	7210
2 skeins	orange yellow	7436
2 skeins	very dark green	7408
3 skeins	jade green	7909
10 skeins	black	

Tapestry needle, size 22.

80 cm (31½ in) black medium-weight cotton
fabric for assembling the cushion.

30 cm (11¾ in) maroon medium-weight
cotton fabric for the piping.

3 m (3¼ yd) cotton piping cord.

Size of finished embroidery: 25 x 25 cm
(10 x 10 in).

Instructions

Prepare and mount the canvas on to a roller
frame as shown in the General Instructions on
page 94.

Measure 10 cm (4 in) in and 10 cm (4 in)
down from the top left-hand corner of the
canvas. This point corresponds with the top
left-hand stitch on the chart. Start the
embroidery here. One square on the chart
represents one stitch on the canvas. Each
symbol represents a colour of the tapestry
wool as shown on the key to the chart.

Work the canvas using half cross-stitch as
illustrated in Needlepoint Techniques on
page 100.

When the stitching is complete, block the
canvas following directions on page 95, and
make up the embroidery into a framed, piped
cushion. Instructions for making up the
cushion are given on page 98.

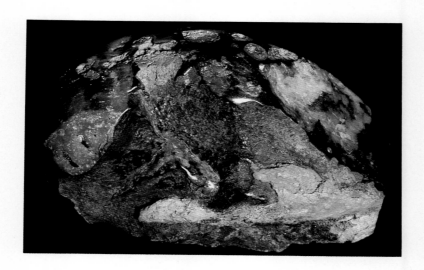

BLACK OPAL

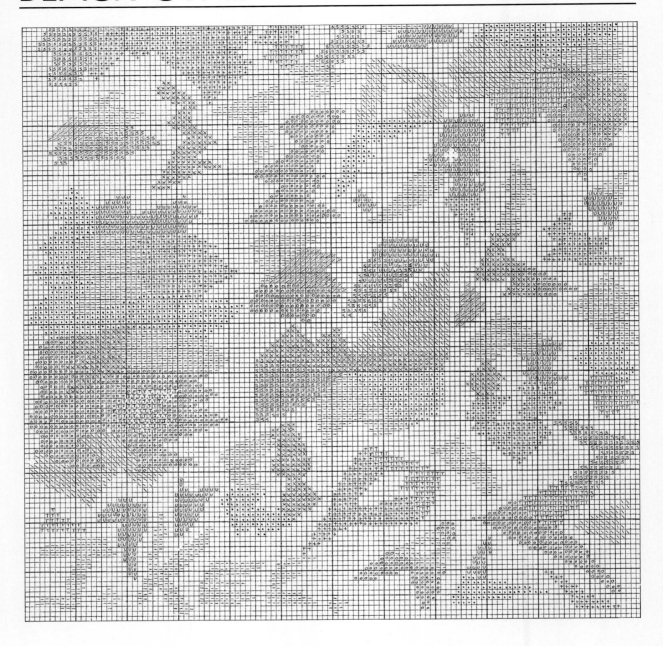

KEY

○	7317
U	7725
—	7544
╲	7708
S	7336
●	7139
X	7210
T	7436
▨	7408
+	7909
☐	black

EARTH DREAMING

Materials

Zweigart canvas 48 threads/10 cm (12 threads/in), a piece 60 x 70 cm (23²/₃ x 27²/₃ in).

DMC Tapestry Wool Article 486 in the following colours and quantities:

7 skeins orange	7850
17 skeins black	
7 skeins yellow	7725
14 skeins red	7108

Tapestry needle, size 22.

Size of finished embroidery: 39.6 x 49.6 cm (15²/₃ x 19½ in).

Note: every stool is different and the embroiderer may be fortunate enough to find one exactly the right size. If unable to do so, complete the embroidery and take it to a specialist needlework shop where you can be directed to a manufacturer of wooden stools.

Instructions

Prepare the canvas as set out in the General Instructions on page 94. The top of the embroidery will be one of the short sides of the canvas. Mount the short sides of the canvas on to the tapes on the roller frame as shown in the General Instructions on page 94.

Measure 10 cm (4 in) in and 10 cm (4 in) down from the top left-hand corner of the canvas. This point corresponds with the top left-hand stitch on the chart. Start the embroidery here. One square on the chart represents one stitch on the canvas. Each symbol represents a colour of the tapestry wool as shown on the key to the chart.

Work the canvas using cross-stitch as shown in Needlepoint Techniques on page 100. Each cross-stitch will cover a two-thread square on the canvas.

When the stitching is complete, block the canvas following directions on page 95, and have it professionally upholstered on to a stool.

EARTH DREAMING

KEY

•	7850
╱	black
○	7725
	7108

65

Harmony

URBAN IMAGE

Materials

Zweigart canvas 48 threads/10 cm
(12 threads/in), a piece 47 x 47 cm
(18½ x 18½ in).

DMC Tapestry Wool Article 486 in the
following colours and quantities:

2 skeins pink	7135
3 skeins red brown	7447
3 skeins bright blue	7995
1 skein yellow	7726
3 skeins white	
3 skeins very dark green	7999
2 skeins bright green	7385
4 skeins mustard yellow	7473
3 skeins aqua	7813
2 skeins crimson	7107
2 skeins wine purple	7228
1 skein dark pink	7137
1 skein jacaranda	7243
4 skeins taupe	7232
2 skeins terracotta	7920
2 skeins black	

Tapestry needle, size 22.

70 cm (27²/3 in) Lincoln green medium-
weight cotton fabric for assembling the
cushion.

30 cm (11¾ in) warm red medium-weight
cotton fabric for the piping.

1.5 m (1²/3 yd) cotton piping cord.

Size of finished embroidery: 27 x 27 cm
(10²/3 x 10²/3 in).

Instructions

Prepare and mount the canvas on to a roller
frame as shown in the General Instructions on
page 94.

Measure 10 cm (4 in) in and 10 cm (4 in)
down from the top left-hand corner of the
canvas. This point corresponds with the top
left-hand stitch on the chart. Start the
embroidery here. One square on the chart
represents one stitch on the canvas. Each
symbol represents a colour of the tapestry
wool as shown on the key to the chart.

Work the canvas using half cross-stitch as
shown in Needlepoint Techniques on
page 100.

When the stitching is complete, block the
canvas following directions on page 95, and
make up the embroidered canvas into a
framed, piped cushion as shown on page 98.

PEACE

KEY

△	black
╱	7316
☐	7136
○	7317
✕	7640
•.	7439
•	7314
+	7726
<	7243
V	7107
╲	7895
⌂	7807
T	7245
S	7155
Z	7153

PAX JOY

Materials

Zweigart canvas 48 threads/10 cm
(12 threads/in), a piece 52 x 57 cm
(20½ x 22½ in).

DMC Tapestry Wool Article 486 in the
following colours and quantities:

3 skeins black		
5 skeins white		
5 skeins red	7666	
2 skeins pink	7603	
4 skeins mid blue	7797	
5 skeins yellow	7435	
5 skeins bright green	7943	
4 skeins jacaranda	7711	
3 skeins royal blue	7319	
5 skeins turquoise	7861	
5 skeins salmon	7951	

Tapestry needle, size 22.

50 cm (19¾ in) bright green medium-weight
cotton fabric for backing the cushion.

30 cm (11¾ in) red medium-weight cotton
fabric for the piping.

1.8 m (2 yd) cotton piping cord.

Size of finished embroidery: 32 x 37 cm
(12²/₃ x 14²/₃ in).

Instructions

Prepare the canvas as set out in the General
Instructions on page 94. The top of the
canvas will be one of the shorter edges of the
canvas. Mount the canvas on to a roller frame
by attaching the shorter edges of the canvas
to the tapes on the frame, following the
instructions on page 94.

Measure 10 cm (4 in) in and 10 cm (4 in)
down from the top left-hand corner of the
canvas. This point corresponds with the top
left-hand stitch on the chart. Start the
embroidery here. One square on the chart
represents one stitch on the canvas. Each
symbol represents a colour of the tapestry
wool as shown on the key to the chart.

Work the canvas using half cross-stitch as
shown in Needlepoint Techniques on page
100.

When the stitching is complete, block the
canvas following directions on page 95, and
make up the embroidery into a piped cushion
according to the instructions on page 99.

PAX JOY

KEY

◢	black
◣	white
☐	7666
•	7603
○	7797
✕	7435
I	7943
╱	7711
−	7319
■	7861
U	7951

DOVES

Materials
Zweigart canvas 48 threads/10 cm
(12 threads/in), a piece 58 x 58 cm
(22¾ x 22¾ in).

DMC Tapestry Wool Article 486 in the
following colours and quantities:

12 skeins midnight blue	7299
14 skeins white	
14 skeins red	7666
4 skeins lavender	7244
2 skeins peacock	7861
1 skein emerald	7345
2 skeins regal	7155
1 skein black	

Tapestry needle, size 22.

Size of finished embroidery: 37.5 x 39.5 cm
(14¾ in x 15½ in).

Instructions
Prepare and mount the canvas on to a roller
frame as shown on page 94. Measure 10 cm
(4 in) in and 10 cm (4 in) down from the top
left-hand corner of the canvas. This point
corresponds with the top left-hand stitch on
the chart. Start the embroidery here. Use half
cross-stitch as shown in Needlepoint
Techniques on page 100. *Note:* the area on
the lower left-hand side of the chart (where
the squares are blank) is not embroidered.
This is where the embroiderer's selected
picture will be placed when the embroidery is
framed.

When the embroidery is complete, block
the canvas following directions on page 95,
and frame it as required.

DOVES

KEY

T	7299
	white
⊞	7666
	7244
◸	7861
⊡	7345
⊠	7155
•	black

MALI

Materials

Zweigart canvas 48 threads/10 cm
(12 threads/in), two pieces as follows:
Chair Seat — cut 1 piece of canvas
71 x 64.5 cm (28 x 25½ in).
Chair Back — cut 1 piece of canvas
88 x 40.5 cm (34²/₃ x 16 in).

DMC Tapestry Wool Article 487* in the
following colours and quantities:

Black	11 hanks
White	3 hanks

(*DMC Tapestry Wool Article 487 is ideal for
working large areas of colour.)

Tapestry needle, size 22.

1.5 m (1²/₃ yd) black cotton gaberdine fabric
for backing embroidery.

1 black director's chair frame.

Size of finished embroideries:
Chair seat — 45 cm (17¾ in) across
x 40.5 cm (16 in) front to back.
Chair back — 64 cm (25¼ in) across
x 16.5 cm (6½ in) high.

Instructions

Prepare and mount the canvas on to a roller
frame as shown in the General Instructions on
page 94. *Note:* a roller frame with long
beams, approximately 90–100 cm
(35½–40 in) long, will be required.

Chair Back: Hold the canvas so one of the
long sides is across the top. Measure 12 cm
(4¾ in) in and 12 cm (4¾ in) down from the
top left-hand corner of the canvas. This point
corresponds with the top left-hand corner of
the chair seat graph. Start the embroidery
here. One square on the chart represents
one stitch on the needlepoint embroidery.
Work the ● symbol on the chart with the white
wool and the blank squares on the chart with
the black wool. The colours may be reversed
if an opposite effect is required.

Work the embroidery in half cross-stitch as
shown in Needlepoint Techniques on page
100.

Chair Seat: Hold the canvas so that one of
the long sides is across the top. Measure
12 cm (4¾ in) in and 12 cm (4¾ in) down
from the top left-hand corner of the canvas.
This point corresponds with the top left-hand
corner of the embroidery graph. Start the
embroidery here.

When both pieces of embroidery are
complete, block the canvases following
directions on page 95, and have them
mounted onto the director's chair frame,
using the black gaberdine fabric as a backing
for the needlepoint.

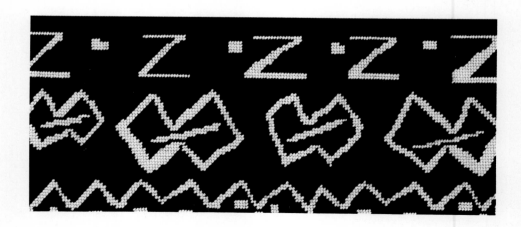

MALI

KEY
☐ black
⊡ white

87

MALI

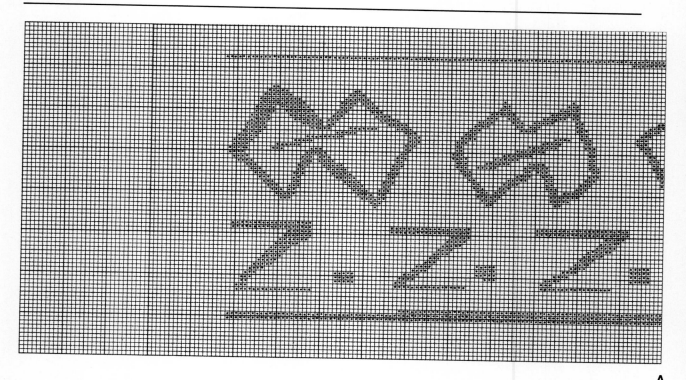

A

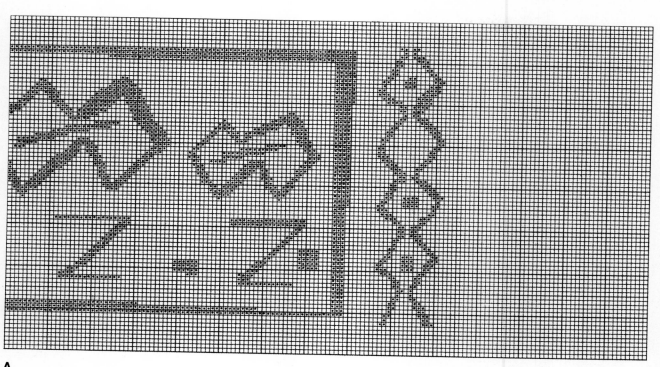

A

join A to A

MASK

Materials

Zweigart canvas 48 threads/10 cm
(12 threads/in), a piece 54 x 60 cm
(21¼ x 23⅔ in).

DMC Tapestry Wool Article 486 in the
following colours and quantities:

22 skeins black	
3 skeins red	7107
2 skeins jacaranda	7711
5 skeins orange	7439
3 skeins purple	7895
1 skein hot pink	7602
3 skeins yellow	7973
3 skeins blue	7316

Tapestry needle, size 22.

40 cm (15¾ in) black medium-weight cotton
fabric for backing table centre.

Size of finished embroidery: 33 x 40 cm
(13 x 15¾ in).

Instructions

Prepare and mount the canvas on to a roller
frame as shown in the General Instructions on
page 94.

Measure 10 cm (4 in) in and 10 cm (4 in)
down from the top left-hand corner of the
canvas. This point corresponds with the top
left-hand stitch on the chart. Start the
embroidery here. One square on the chart
represents one stitch on the canvas. Each
symbol represents a colour of the tapestry
wool as shown on the key to the chart.

Work the canvas using half cross-stitch as
shown in Needlepoint Techniques on page
100.

When the stitching is complete, block the
canvas following directions on page 95, and
make up the embroidery by trimming away
the excess canvas so that there are only 8
unworked threads remaining around the
outside of the embroidery on each of the four
sides of the table centre. Turn the unworked
canvas to the back of the work so that the last
black row of stitching is sitting on the edge of
the work. Pin and herringbone stitch the
unworked canvas to the back of the
embroidery using black thread. Make sure
that the herringbone stitches do not go
through the embroidery to the right side of
the work.

From the black backing fabric, cut a piece
of fabric which is 2 cm (¾ in) larger on all four
sides than the hemmed embroidery. Place
the embroidery in the middle of the backing
fabric with wrong sides together and turn in
the edges of the backing fabric so that the
backing sits neatly behind the embroidery
and no white canvas is showing. Pin the two
layers together around the outside and slip-
stitch the folds together using black thread.

MASK

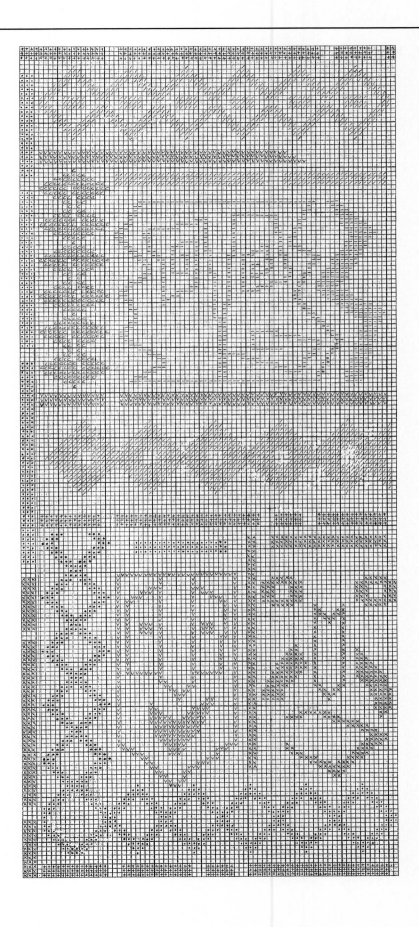

KEY

☐	black
╱	7107
+	7711
•	7439
V	7895
c	7602
—	7973
✕	7316

General Instructions

MOUNTING A CANVAS

Canvas Preparation

Cover the edges of the cut canvas with 2.5 cm (1 in) masking tape so that the tape is folded around the cut edge of the canvas. This simple procedure prevents the canvas fraying and the tapestry wool becoming snagged in the cut threads at the edge.

Measure the top and bottom sides of the canvas with a tape measure and mark the centre of each side using a laundry marker pen or indelible pen.

Roller Frame Preparation

Using a tape measure, find the centre of the cotton tape attached to the two long beams of the roller frame. Mark each centre point with a laundry marker pen. These centre point markings will be used for each piece of canvas mounted on the frame.

Match the centre mark of one edge of the canvas to the centre mark on the cotton tape on the frame. Thread a large chenille needle (a tapestry needle with a sharp point) with strong thread and sew the canvas to the cotton tape using a running stitch. The running stitch does not have to be small — a stitch length of 1 cm ($\frac{1}{3}$ in) is fine, but the canvas and tape must be joined so that they lie straight and even.

Join the opposite end of the canvas to the other long beam on the frame in the same manner. When the canvas is attached to the frame and rolled around the long beams, the cotton tape should lie flat and smooth around each beam. Check that this will happen prior to stitching the second side of the canvas to the second beam by pinning the canvas to the cotton tape and rolling the canvas around the beam.

Assemble the roller frame by placing a side beam at each end of the long beams, so forming a rectangular frame. Roll the canvas around one of the beams. Tighten the canvas around the long beams and use the wing nuts supplied with the frame to hold the canvas firmly in place.

A superior result will be achieved if the canvas is laced to each of the side beams holding the canvas taut within the frame. Thread a chenille needle with approximately 2 m ($2\frac{1}{4}$ yd) strong thread (e.g., linen thread, light string or fine nylon knitting wool). Tie one end securely to one side of the canvas and pass the threaded needle through the canvas and around the outside of the adjacent side beam. Bring the needle up through the canvas about 1.5 cm ($\frac{1}{2}$ in) away from the knot and take the thread around the outside of the side beam again. Repeat until the end of the canvas is reached, pull the lacing tight, and work a few stitches in one spot at the edge of the canvas to finish off. Lace the other side beam in the same manner. The lacing may need tightening periodically as the embroidery proceeds.

Start to embroider the canvas so that the right side of the work lies within the recession of the roller frame. In this way when the canvas is rolled around the beams, the wrong side of the embroidery will be outermost keeping the right side of the work clean and undisturbed.

When the canvas is ready to be rolled on, undo the lacings, release the tension on the wing nuts, re-roll the canvas tightly and replace the side lacings to ensure an even work tension is maintained.

Hint: When selecting a roller frame, a 75 cm ($29\frac{1}{2}$ in) or 90 cm (1 yd) wide frame will suit most pieces of work in this book.

A frame of this size will also be comfortable to work on as it will sit easily across the arms of a chair allowing the embroiderer to have both hands free to stitch.

Two-Handed Technique

The two-handed technique is ideal when embroidering on a roller frame. The stitcher should keep the hand with which they write underneath the frame and the other hand on the top of the frame. The embroidery is worked by passing the needle through the canvas from one hand to the other. The two-handed technique allows the embroiderer to maintain a comfortable posture in a chair without having to support the weight of the frame and it allows both hands to control the needle and thread without having to hold on to the frame. With practice the technique will result in fast, evenly tensioned embroidery.

Persevere — it is worthwhile!

The roller frame may be mounted on to a floor stand and the two-handed technique followed as set out above.

Hint: When starting a canvas, use a pencil and write TOP along the top edge of the canvas. This will help to identify where to re-start the embroidery when the canvas is picked up after being left for a period of time.

BLOCKING

Blocking is the simple process of straightening and smoothing out the completed needlepoint before it is assembled into its finished form. It is important never to iron needlepoint as the heat will break down the sizing, which gives stiffness to the canvas.

Blocking is important for three reasons. First, it will restore an out-of-shape piece to its original shape. Secondly, it will smooth out any minor stitching irregularities and thirdly, it will redistribute the sizing in the canvas firming up the needlepoint.

All needlepoint should be blocked and if the embroiderer finds this process too difficult or inconvenient, specialist needlework shops will be able to provide a blocking service.

The following equipment is required:

1. a piece of solid timber (not chipboard, particle board or cork) which is approximately 10 cm (4 in) larger on each side than the canvas to be blocked and approximately 1.6 cm (⅝ in) thick.
2. 2.5 cm (1 in) nails (drawing pins may be used but they are difficult to press into the canvas and board and more difficult to remove later).
3. a hammer.
4. a tape measure.
5. a water spray.

Needlepoint which is not textured should be blocked with the right side facing the board. The After the Fire pattern should be blocked with the right side up so that the French knots will not be flattened. All other needlepoint in this book should be blocked with the right side facing the board.

Spray the back of the finished embroidery with water from the water spray before it is nailed to the board. The canvas should not be saturated, just moistened to soften and allow it to be stretched and straightened.

Lay the canvas on to the blocking board according to the directions above. Starting from one corner, nail the canvas to the board through the masking tape around the edge. The nails should be placed at intervals of approximately 1.3 cm (½ in) and will need only four or five firm taps — they should not be hammered right into the board. Check that the edge of the canvas is parallel to the edge of the board. Go back to the corner of the canvas which was attached first and work down the other side, using the tape measure to check that the edge of the canvas is parallel to the edge of the board. The canvas should be taut between each nail.

The remaining two sides of the canvas should be attached by stretching the canvas taut so that it is parallel to the edge of the board. Along one unnailed side, hammer in a few nails at 1.3 cm (½ in) intervals and then insert a few nails along the other unnailed side. Alternate from one side to the other until the entire canvas is nailed to the board.

The board and canvas should then be placed in an airy position, not in the sun, until the canvas is totally dry. It usually takes two or three days for the canvas to dry, although in humid weather it might take longer.

When the canvas is dry, use the claw end of the hammer to remove the nails. If they were not hammered in too hard, they should be easy to withdraw from the board. Once the canvas is removed from the blocking board it should be made up into its finished article without delay. If the canvas was badly out of shape prior to blocking and the project is not made up immediately, the needlepoint may revert to its distorted shape.

ASSEMBLING CUSHIONS

The assembly of a needlepoint project is just as important as the needlepoint itself. Many embroiderers find the making up of a project daunting as it can be a complicated procedure. Instructions for the assembly of a piped cushion and a framed, piped cushion are given below, but if you find them more than you can handle, take your completed project, and the backing and piping fabric along to a specialist needlework shop. Most specialist needlework shops either provide such a service or can recommend one.

Piping

Piping is the covered cotton cord around the outside of all the cushions in this book. It provides an attractive contrasting, but defined edge to the needlepoint and, perhaps more importantly, gives structural support to the shape of the project.

When making a length of piping with which to trim needlepoint, always make a length which is about 20 cm (7¾ in) longer than the perimeter length of the project so that the ends can be joined and finished off neatly. For example, if a cushion is 1.5 m (1⅔ yd) around the outer edge of the embroidery, make a length of piping which is 1.7 m (1¾ yd) long.

Instructions

Wash, dry and press the piping fabric and lay it out flat on a table. Starting at one selvedge, measure 30 cm (11¾ in) in along the cut edge and mark this point with a pencil. Measure along the selvedge for 30 cm (11¾ in) and mark this point with a pencil. Using a ruler, join the two points with a line.

This newly drawn line will be the true bias of the fabric. Holding the ruler at right angles to the drawn line, measure 5 cm (2 in) at two points along the true bias. Using the ruler, connect the two points marked with a pencil line. Continue measuring and ruling off lengths of bias until there are enough ruled strips to go around the perimeter of the cushion plus about 20 cm (7¾ in). *Figure 1* shows how to draw up the strips.

Cut the strips of bias along the drawn lines, leaving each in position flat on the table as it is cut. Pick up the top end of the first strip and place its right side facing the right side of the bottom end of the strip alongside, as shown in *Figure 2*. Notice that in order to have the ends of each strip together, one strip will have to come in from the left and the other strip will have to come in from the right. Keeping the ends of the strips even, slide the strips across one another until the bottom of the 'V' shape formed at the side, see *Figure 2*, is 1 cm (⅓ in) from the end of the strips. Pin the strips together as shown in *Figure 2*.

Pin all the strips together to make one continuous length of piping bias, checking that all the right sides are facing the same way. Stitch between the bottom of the 'V' at one end of a strip and the bottom of the 'V' at the other end of the strip as shown in *Figure 2*. Stitch together all the lengths of bias in this manner. Press seam allowances open.

Fold the bias around the piping cord as shown in *Figure 3*. Pin and, using the zipper foot on the sewing machine, stitch the bias around the piping cord making sure that the stitching is very close to the cord.

Figure 1
Cutting the bias strips

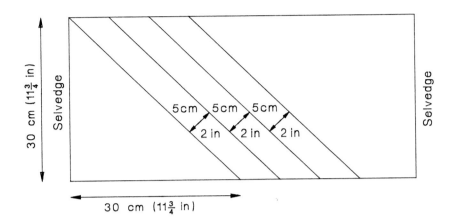

30 cm (11¾ in)

Selvedge

5cm 5cm 5cm

2 in 2 in 2 in

Selvedge

30 cm (11¾ in)

Figure 2
Joining the bias strips

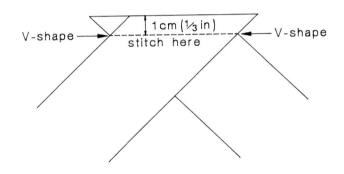

V-shape

1 cm (⅓ in)
stitch here

V-shape

Figure 3
Folding and stitching the piping

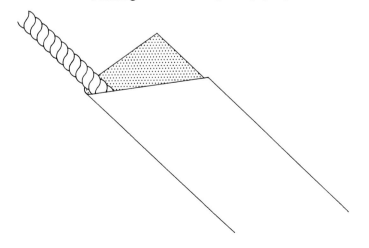

MAKING UP A FRAMED, PIPED CUSHION

All of the framed cushions in this book have a 5-cm (2-in) wide frame. To cut out the frame, measure the sides of the cushion and cut four strips, one for each side of the cushion. Each strip should measure the length of one side plus 14 cm (5½ in). Each strip should be 9 cm (3½ in) wide. The measurements given include a seam allowance of 2 cm (¾ in).

Sew the long end of a strip to the edge of the embroidery so that the strip extends 7 cm (2¾ in) beyond the edge of the embroidery on each side. Stop the stitching precisely at the edge of the embroidery. Repeat for the remaining three sides. When each side of the embroidery has a frame strip sewn to it, join

the edges with the aid of a set square, so that they will form a mitre. Before stitching a mitred seam, pin it and then open it back to check that the frame lies smoothly. If the frame does not lie as it should, go back to the set square and adjust the pins.

When the four mitred corners are sewn, trim the seam allowance on the canvas to 1.5 cm (½ in). Following the instructions for piping on page 96, cut out and prepare the piping for the cushion and attach it to the frame strips 5 cm (2 in) from the seam where the embroidery joins the frame. Complete the cushion following the steps given for making up a piped cushion.

MAKING UP A PIPED CUSHION

After a cushion has been blocked and is completely dry, remove it from the blocking board. Measure the length of piping required for the cushion and make it according to the instructions given on page 96.

Start pinning the piping to the needlepoint halfway along the bottom edge, leaving about 5 cm (2 in) of piping unattached at the start. The outer, raw edges of the piping should face the same way as the outer, unworked edge of the embroidery. The cord side of the piping should face the centre of the cushion.

For the piping to lie smoothly around the corners, carefully snip the seam allowance on the piping several times so that when it is pinned around a corner, the seam allowance lies flat against the unworked canvas. Do not make a right-angled corner with the piping, rather have a gently rounded curve.

Continue pinning the piping to the needlepoint until the beginning is reached. Unpick about 5 cm (2 in) of the stitching holding the cord in the bias at each end. Pin the two ends of the bias together at the point where it is the right length to lie flat on the surface of the cushion. Sew the two ends of bias together, with the piping cord out of the way. Trim the seam allowance and press open. Fold the joined bias strip around the piping cord once more, overlapping the ends of the cord together within the bias. Keeping the piping clear of the embroidered cushion cover, stitch the cord into the bias, keeping the stitching very close to the cord. Pin the joined piping into position on the needlepoint. Using a zipper foot, machine sew the piping to the needlepoint all around, making sure that the stitching is very close to the cord.

From the cushion backing fabric, cut a piece which is 10 cm (4 in) larger than the needlepoint's overall measurement, for example, if the finished embroidery is 35 x 35 cm (13¾ x 13¾ in), cut the backing fabric 45 x 45 cm (17¾ x 17¾ in). With the right side of the needlepoint facing the right side of the backing, pin the two layers together close to but on the outer edge of the piping. Using the zipper foot, machine sew along the line of pins leaving a gap of at least 20 cm (8 in) in the middle of the one side of the cushion.

Trim the seam allowances to 1.5 cm (½ in). On the sewing machine, zigzag stitch along all raw edges. Turn the cushion right side out. Push a cushion insert through the opening and slip-stitch closed.

Note: a cushion insert should always be 2.5 cm (1 in) larger than the finished overall measurement of the cushion, for example, if the finished cushion is 35 x 35 cm (13¾ x 13¾ in), the insert should be 37.5 x 37.5 cm (14¾ x 14¾ in).

NEEDLEPOINT TECHNIQUES

Two-handed Technique
See page 94 for instructions.

Half Cross-stitch

Half cross-stitch can be worked from left to right or from right to left by following the step-by-step instructions in *Figures 4* and *5*.

On whichever side a row is started the stitch should appear as an oblique which slopes from lower left to upper right. The back of the work should show a vertical stitch as shown in *Figure 6*, except when rows are being changed or when a colour is broken by another colour or colours. *Note:* when working a broken area of one colour do not jump across more than two or three stitches at the back of the work.

Starting with a waste knot as shown in *Figure 7* is fast and neat. Measure 10 cm (4 in) in and 10 cm (4 in) down from the top left-hand corner of the canvas. This is point A which corresponds with the top left-hand stitch on the chart. Using a 30 cm (11¾ in) length of the correct tapestry wool colour according to the chart, thread through a tapestry needle and tie a knot at the end. Take the needle down through the canvas five or six threads to the right of point A. The knot should be on the right side of the canvas. Bring the needle up to the right side on the same horizontal row at point A. The next five or six stitches should cover the starting thread at the back of the work. When the stitching reaches the knot, simply cut the knot off from the right side of the embroidery taking care not to cut the actual embroidery.

To end off a thread, finish the stitch at the back of the canvas and run the needle underneath five or six vertical backs of half cross-stitches, as shown in *Figure 8*. Cut off excess thread close to the surface of the canvas. If the excess thread has not been trimmed any little tails left behind are likely to be pulled through to the front of the embroidery and will look unsightly.

Cross-stitch

Three projects are worked in cross-stitch on the same type of canvas as the others, but because each stitch is worked over an

Figure 4
Half cross-stitch — row worked from left to right

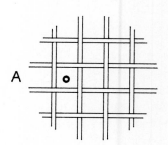

A

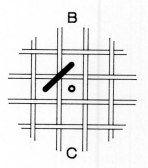

B

C

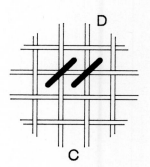

D

C

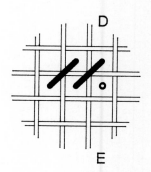

D

E

Figure 5
Half cross-stitch — row worked from right to left

A

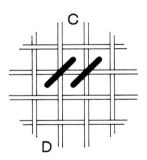

C

B

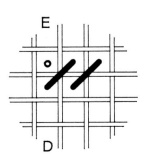

C

D

E

D

Figure 6
Half cross-stitch — back of the work

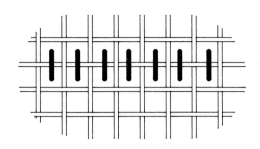

Figure 7
Starting with a waste knot

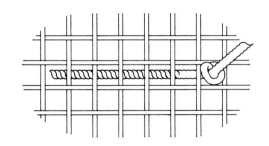

Figure 8
To end off a thread

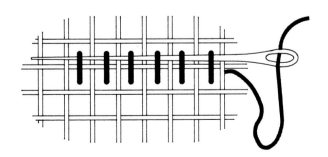

NEEDLEPOINT TECHNIQUES

Figure 9
Cross-stitch

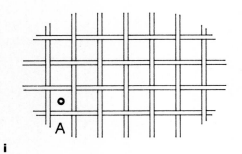

i

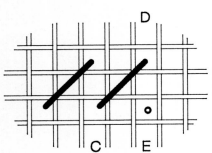

ii

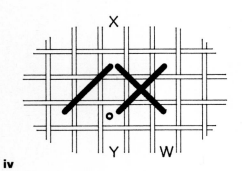

iii

iv

v

Figure 10
French knot

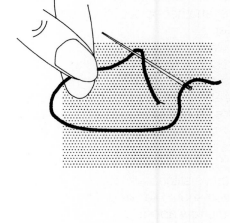

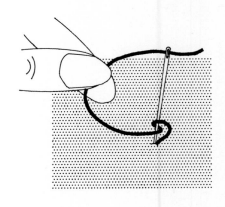

imaginary square of two threads high and two threads wide the stitch size is larger.

Thread the tapestry needle with one strand of the required tapestry wool colour approximately 40 cm (15¾ in) long. Start with a waste knot as shown in *Figure 7* on page 101. Work the stitch by bringing the needle out of the canvas at the lower left hand side of the imaginary square (see *Figure 9i*) at point A. Count two threads to the right and two threads up and push the needle down through the canvas at point B. Bring the needle up through to the right side of the canvas two threads below B at point C (see *Figure 9ii*). Count two threads to the right and two threads up and push the needle down through the canvas at point D (see *Figure 9iii*). Continue in this manner until the row contains as many stitches in the threaded colour as shown on the area to be worked on the chart. Do not jump more than three stitches of another colour. Work these other areas later.

Next, work back across the row from right to left crossing the half crosses to complete the cross-stitches according to the illustrations in *Figure 9iv* and *9v*. Notice that the second part of the cross-stitch is worked into the same holes in the canvas as the first part of the cross-stitch.

Do not miss a line of canvas between two rows of cross-stitches. In every row, each cross-stitch should lie directly beneath the stitch in the row above.

French Knots

Thread the needle with one strand of tapestry wool in the correct colour. Bring the needle to the right side of the embroidery in the place where the French knot is required and pull the wool through the fabric ready to start the stitch. For right-handed embroiderers, hold the thread about 2.5 cm (1 in) away from the surface of the fabric with the left hand. Hold the needle with the right hand, pointing it up away from the surface of the fabric. Wrap the thread around the needle once or twice, see *Figure 10i*. Still holding the thread taut in the left hand and not letting go of the needle, turn the needle down to face the surface of the fabric and push the point of the needle into the fabric a very short distance from where the thread is emerging, see *Figure 10ii*. Do not push the needle back into the same hole where the thread is coming through, as then the French knot is likely to pull through the fabric to the wrong side. As the needle is pushed into the fabric, pull the thread in the left hand so that there is no slack left in it and the knot is sitting on the surface of the fabric. Only at this stage is the needle pulled all the way through to the back of the embroidery.

If the embroiderer is left handed, simply follow the same instructions above, substituting left hand for right and vice versa.